UNDERSTANDING SCIENCE

MAGNETISM

PUBLISHED BY SMART APPLE MEDIA

1980 Lookout Drive, North Mankato, Minnesota 56003

PHOTOGRAPHS by Bonnie Sue, Richard Goff, Tom Myers, Photo Researchers (Library of Congress, Science Source, David Parker, Science Photo Library), Photri-Microstock, Rainbow Photography (Coco McCoy), Tom Stack & Associates (NCAR/TSADO), D. Jeanene Tiner, Unicorn Stock Photos (Richard Gilbert, Tom McCarthy)

DESIGN AND PRODUCTION Evansday Design

LIBRARY OF CONGRESS CATALOGING-IN-PUBLICATION DATA

Tiner, John Hudson, 1944–
Magnetism / by John Hudson Tiner.
p. cm. — (Understanding science)
Includes index.

Summary: Examines the force of magnetism and describes the properties and uses of magnets.

ISBN 1-58340-158-X
1. Magnets—Juvenile literature. 2. Magnetism—Juvenile literature. [1. Magnets. 2. Magnetism.] I. Title. II. Series.

QC757.5 .T56 2002

538'.4—dc21   2001054986

First Edition

9 8 7 6 5 4 3 2 1

Magnetism

[John Hudson Tiner]

MAGNETS HAVE MANY SURPRISING PROPERTIES. WHEN A MAGNET IS BROUGHT CLOSE TO A PAPER CLIP MADE OF IRON, THE PAPER CLIP JUMPS UP TO THE MAGNET. YET THE SAME MAGNET LEAVES UNMOVED PIECES OF WOOD, GLASS, OR PLAS- TIC. FOR THOUSANDS OF YEARS, PEOPLE HAVE ENJOYED LEARNING ABOUT THE FASCINATING PROPERTIES OF MAGNETS, AND SCIENTISTS HAVE FOUND A WIDE ARRAY OF USES FOR MAGNETS AND MAGNETISM.

Thales (THAY-leez) was a Greek scientist who lived about 2,500 years ago. He experimented with an unusual iron **ore** that could pick up iron objects but not other metals. The iron ore was named magnetite because it was first discovered in a region in Turkey called Magnesia. Later, scientists learned that if they suspended magnetite from a string, it always swung around to point north and south. Magnetite became known as lodestone, a word meaning "leading stone." The first crude compass for telling direction was made by hanging lodestone from a string. One end pointed north, and the other end pointed south. Scientists did not know what caused the magnetite to point along a north-south line. Some thought it was Polaris, the North Star. An iron needle could be made magnetic by stroking it with lodestone. Putting a magnetized needle on a **pivot** made a better compass. In 1492,

*An **ore** is a mineral that contains a metal that can be mined and extracted at a profit.*

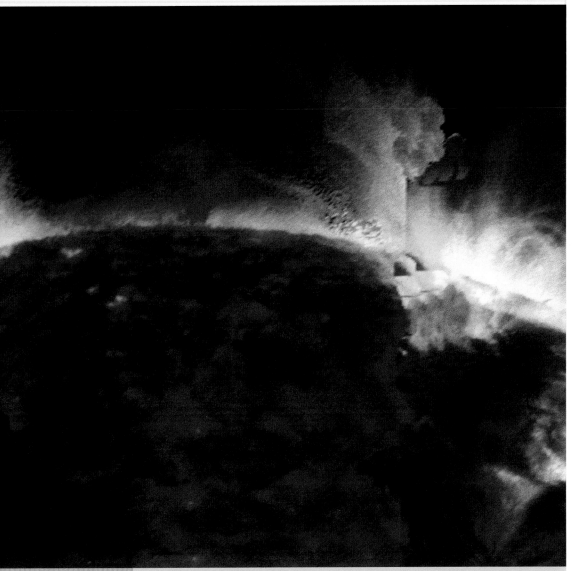

CHARGED PARTICLES FROM THE SUN ARE SUSCEPTIBLE TO MAGNETISM

Storms on the surface of the sun shoot tiny, electrically charged particles into space. Earth's magnetism attracts them as they pass near our planet. The particles crash into the atmosphere and create a glow known as the northern lights.

Christopher Columbus used such a compass when he sailed to the New World. William Gilbert, a doctor who lived in London in the late 1500s, discovered why a compass pointed north. Gilbert made a dip compass: one with a needle that could turn up and down. When he released the needle, he expected it to rise and point into the sky toward the North Star. To his astonishment, it pointed down at the ground. The needle aimed for a point below the horizon thousands of miles away from London.

*A **helmsman** is a person who steers a ship.*

In the 1500s, captains of ships believed that garlic would damage the magnetic properties of a compass. The British navy took the idea seriously. Any **helmsman** who came on duty with garlic breath was subject to flogging.

The **geographic North Pole** *is the point on the earth's surface marking the axis around which the earth rotates.*

A TIME-LAPSE PHOTO OF THE NIGHT SKY DIRECTLY OVER THE NORTH POLE

"The compass points north because Earth itself is a magnet," Gilbert concluded. It was later discovered that one of the points that attracts a magnet is located in Canada about 1,100 miles (1,760 km) from the **geographic North Pole**. The other point is located near the South Pole in Antarctica.

A bar magnet is a straight iron rod with a north magnetic pole at one end and a south magnetic pole at the other end. A magnet's attraction is strongest at its poles. Suppose a magnet is rolled around in iron tacks. More tacks will cluster around each of the poles than in the middle. **The unlike poles of two magnets will attract one another. That is, a north pole of one magnet will attract the south pole of another magnet. But like poles repel, or push away from each other. A north pole repels a north pole, and a south pole repels a south pole.** A bar made of pure iron will become magnetic while in contact with a magnet. But when the magnet is removed, the iron bar loses its magnetism. It is a **temporary magnet**. Steel is an **alloy** of iron. It is made of iron, carbon, and other metals. Steel can be made into a magnet by stroking it in the same direction 50 to 100 times

A **temporary magnet** *is a metal that becomes magnetic while within a magnetic field but loses its magnetism when removed from the magnetic field.*

MAGNETITE, IRON ORE MADE MAGNETIC BY THE EARTH'S MAGNETISM

A horseshoe magnet is U-shaped. The poles are across from one another and work together to lift heavy objects. Police sometimes use horseshoe magnets on the end of ropes to search lake bottoms for weapons used in crimes.

with a strong magnet. Once it becomes magnetized, it does not easily lose its magnetism. It becomes a **permanent magnet**. Compass needles are made of steel. All substances are made of tiny particles known as atoms. The smallest bit of iron is an iron atom. Scientists have found that in iron and a few other metals, the atoms cluster together in groups called domains. Each domain is a miniature magnet. In most metals, the domains face in every direction and thereby cancel out the magnetic effect of one another. But in magnetic materials, the domains point in the same direction. Their individual magnetic effects add together to make the magnet stronger. All magnets, even permanent magnets, can lose their magnetism. Bar magnets need to be stored so that their poles are north to south. If magnets are forced together

COMPASS NEEDLES ARE MADE OF STEEL THAT HAS BEEN MADE MAGNETIC

north to north and south to south, the repelling poles turn some of the domains around, weakening their magnetic effect. Dropping a magnet on the floor can also jar the domains. Heat is another enemy of magnetism. An iron magnet heated to 1,455 °F (791 °C) will lose its magnetic power. Heat causes the domains to wiggle around so they no longer work together.

In 1819, a Danish science teacher named Christian Oersted tested whether an electric current could produce magnetism. He attached a wire to a battery and ran the wire across a compass. When he turned on the electricity, the compass needle suddenly swung to one side. When he turned off the electricity, the compass needle swung back. Current in the wire did indeed make a magnet. **The space around a magnet is called a magnetic field.** It is the area where the force of a magnet acts. A magnetic field encircles any wire carrying an electric current. William Sturgeon, an English scientist, wound insulated wire into a coil to make the field stronger. Putting an iron bar down the middle of the coil strengthened the magnetic field even more. This type of magnet is called an

*A **magnetic field** is the region around a magnet where its force of attraction or repulsion acts on another magnet or object.*

LARGE ELECTROMAGNETS ARE USED TO SAFELY LIFT HEAVY SCRAP METAL

The metals aluminum, nickel, and cobalt are slightly magnetic. However, when melted together to form alnico, they make one of the strongest permanent magnets known. The word alnico is formed of the first two letters of aluminum, nickel, and cobalt.

electromagnet. Sturgeon made the first electro-magnet in 1825. Within a few years, inventors built electromagnets so strong they could lift heavy loads of scrap metal. Unlike natural magnets, elec-

ELECTROMAGNETS MAKE MOTORS AND MANY OTHER DEVICES POSSIBLE

Electrons *are tiny, electrically charged particles that orbit around the nucleus of an atom.*

tromagnets can be turned on and off. In the 1800s, a communication device called a telegraph made use of this to send messages from one city to another. In one city, a telegraph operator rapidly tapped a key that turned electricity on and off. In another city, the current of electricity passed through an electromagnet. The electromagnet raised and lowered a pen. The pen drew dots and dashes on a strip of paper that passed under the pen. The dots and dashes stood for letters that spelled out a message.

The magnetic field of an electromagnet can be made stronger or weaker by changing the amount of electricity that flows through the wire. Electromagnets control the beam of **electrons** that create the glowing picture on the front of television screens.

Christian Oersted discovered that electricity could produce magnetism. His discovery led other scientists to wonder if it would work the other way. Could magnets be used to generate electricity? The first scientists to experiment with this idea put strong magnets next to wires. No electricity flowed. Michael Faraday, an English scientist who lived in London, tried to make electricity from magnetism for many years. In one experiment, he wrapped a coil of wire around a magnet. He hooked the wire to an electric meter for detecting weak electric currents. No electricity flowed, but Faraday did not give up. One day in 1831, Faraday thrust a bar magnet into the coil of wire while it was hooked to the electric meter. The needle on the electric meter flickered, showing that a small amount of electricity flowed. But the needle quickly fell back. Faraday pulled out the bar magnet. The needle

SAMUEL MORSE REVOLUTIONIZED COMMUNICATION WITH THE TELEGRAPH

Samuel F. B. Morse invented the telegraph. He was also a successful artist
who painted portraits, including those of
United States presidents. Morse became
interested in electricity and sent the first
telegraph message in 1844.

flickered again. Suddenly, he realized that he had found the solution. Motion was the key; a magnetic field must be moving to create electricity. **With this knowledge, Faraday quickly built the first electric generator. By turning a crank, he spun a magnet around inside a coil of wire. As long as he turned the crank, electricity flowed through the wire. Today, rapidly spinning magnets are used in tur‑bines to produce electricity. Electrical lines carry this electricity to businesses, schools, and homes.**

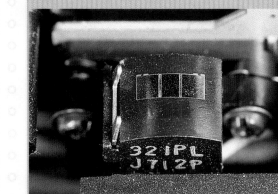

Scientists stir chemicals in a beaker by dropping a magnet inside. They then set the beaker on a machine that has a rotating magnet. The rotating magnet's attraction turns the magnet in the beaker and keeps the contents stirred.

MICHAEL FARADAY'S DISCOVERIES IN ELECTROMAGNETISM CHANGED THE WORLD

Turbines *are machines with vanes or blades that are turned by rapidly moving liquids or gases such as steam or wind.*

People use magnets every day in their businesses or homes. A refrigerator door has a magnetic strip all around it. The door closes against another magnetic strip. The poles on the two strips are opposite. The door makes a firm seal because the opposite poles attract each other. Many people also use the metal front of a refrigerator door as a bulletin board. Photos and notes are held in place by magnets. A cassette recorder uses magnets to capture sound or music. A person speaks or plays music into a microphone. The sound waves cause a magnet to move back and forth, which generates an electric current. The current powers an electromagnet called a recording head. A cassette tape has iron particles embedded in it. The tape passes across the recording head, which makes some of the iron particles magnetic. During playback, the tape passes across a playback head. This time, the

A **short circuit** *is a shortcut across an electric circuit that allows more electricity to flow than the circuit can carry.*

MAGNETS MAKE IT POSSIBLE TO RECORD, STORE, AND PLAY BACK SOUND

A **short circuit** is a dangerous flaw in electric wires. Too much electricity flows. The wires overheat and can start a fire. A circuit breaker is a type of electromagnet. It throws a safety switch that turns off the electricity.

MAGNETS ARE AN INTEGRAL PART OF POWERFUL COMPUTER DRIVES

magnetic iron particles on the tape produce an electric current with the same pattern as the original sound. Speakers or earphones also use electromagnets. An electromagnet rapidly attracts and releases a metal disk to produce sound waves. Computers use hard drives to record large amounts of information. A hard drive is a device that has spinning disks coated with a substance that contains iron. A recording head causes individual spots on the drive to become magnetic when data is recorded. A reading head passes over the magnetic spots to read the data.

Grazing cattle sometimes swallow small pieces of wire and iron that could injure them. Farmers feed the cows magnets that lodge in their stomachs and attract the iron to keep it safely out of the rest of their digestive tracts.

Magnets may be even more important in the future than they are today. One of the forces that rob cars of energy is friction between the tires and the road. Scientists are working on vehicles that float above the road on magnetic fields. This would do away with tires and the friction they cause. Floating trains have already been built and tested. Electromagnets both lift the vehicle above the track and pull it forward. The train zooms along at more than 300 miles (483 km) per hour. Some types of **nuclear reactions** can produce temperatures hotter than the surface of the sun. The hot nuclear material, made of atoms that have melted together, would burn a hole through any container meant to hold it. However, scientists have learned how to make a magnetic bottle to hold the hot material. An invisible magnetic field keeps the hot material from touching anything else. Someday this type of

*__Nuclear reactions__ are changes in the nucleus, or center, of
an atom; nuclear reactions release energy.*

A MODERN ELECTROMAGNETIC PASSENGER TRAIN AT A STATION IN JAPAN

For safety, airline passengers pass
through metal detectors before boarding
airplanes. A metal object such as a knife
or gun causes a change in the magnetic
field and sounds an alarm.

nuclear energy in magnetic bottles may help provide part of the world's energy needs. Some liquids contain **crystals** that turn the same direction when put in a magnetic field. The surface of the substance changes color as if a curtain had been opened or closed. Digital wristwatches and game machines use liquid crystals to display information. In the future, it may be possible to publish an entire newspaper on a single sheet of special paper. A new page would be revealed as the liquid crystals in the paper were turned on and off with magnetism to display a new page of words. Magnetic poles always come in pairs; a north pole and a south pole. Scientists have tried to separate the poles, but so far have not been able to do so. If they cut a magnet in half, each half still has a north and south pole. No matter how many times a magnet is cut, the

LIQUID CRYSTALS CAN BE MOVED BY MAGNETISM TO FORM COLORS AND SHAPES

individual pieces always have both a north and south pole. Today, magnetism is employed for many purposes. Some magnets are easy to notice, such as those found on refrigerator doors. Others are hidden inside devices such as the telephone and television. Although scientists know a lot about magnetism, they still have much more to learn. What remains to be discovered about magnetism may make everyday life easier—and more fun.

THE BEAUTIFUL NORTHERN LIGHTS ARE CREATED BY EARTH'S MAGNETISM

MAGNETISM EXPERIMENT

Iron is attracted by a magnet, while other materials do not respond to a magnet. In this experiment, you will use a magnet to determine whether hidden objects are made of iron or some other material.

WHAT YOU NEED

A magnet

Six small plastic containers (the plastic cans that film comes in will work)

An iron paper clip

An iron washer

An iron nut from a bolt

A rubber eraser

A copper coin

A glass marble

WHAT YOU DO

1. Pass the magnet over the paper clip, washer, and nut to prove that the magnet attracts them.

2. Pass the magnet over the eraser, coin, and marble to prove that the magnet does not attract them.

3. While you are not looking, have a friend hide the objects in the containers.

4. Have your friend give you the containers in these pairs without telling you which one contains which item:

   paper clip and eraser

   washer and coin

   nut and marble

5. Use the magnet to reveal which container in each pair hides the iron object. Open the containers to see if you are correct.

WHAT YOU SEE

The magnet lets you discover which object is hidden inside each container because the magnetic field penetrates the plastic container. The magnetic field attracts iron and steel, but not copper, rubber, or glass.

INDEX

A
alnico, 15

C
cassette recorders, 22
cassette tapes, 22
cattle feed, 25
circuit breakers, 23
compasses, 6, 8-9, 12, 14
computer hard drives, 25

D
domains, 12, 13

E
electricity generation, 18, 20

F
Faraday, Michael, 18, 20
floating trains, 26

G
Gilbert, William, 8-9

L
liquid crystals, 28
lodestone, 6
loss of magnetism, 12-13

M
magnetic bottles, 26, 28
magnetic fields, 14, 17, 20, 26, 27, 31
magnetic poles, 10, 11, 12-13, 22, 28-29
magnetite, 6

magnets, 6, 10, 11, 12, 14, 15, 16, 17, 18, 22, 23, 26
    bar magnets, 10, 12, 18
    electromagnets, 14, 16, 17, 22, 23, 26
    horseshoe magnets, 11
    making magnets, 6, 10, 12, 14, 16
    permanent magnets, 12, 15
    temporary magnets, 10, 11
metal detectors, 27
mixing chemicals, 20
Morse, Samuel F. B., 19

N
northern lights, 7

O
Oersted, Christian, 14, 18

R
refrigerator doors, 22

S
speakers, 25
Sturgeon, William, 14, 16

T
telegraph, 17, 19
Thales, 6